Fisher-Friedman Associates
Associates
FFA

In Praise of Pragmatism
1964-2000
2000-2010

Foreword by
Frank Anton

Introduction by
John T. Friedman, FAIA

Essay by
Daniel Solomon, FAIA

ORO

Contents

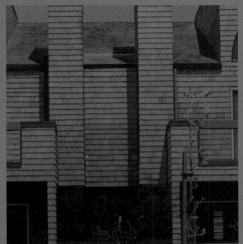  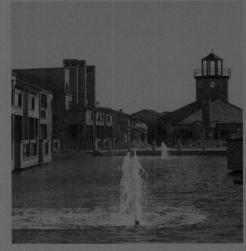
 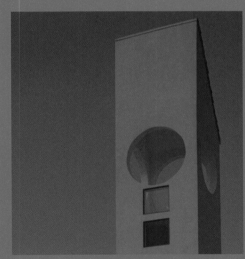 
  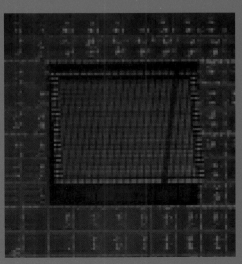

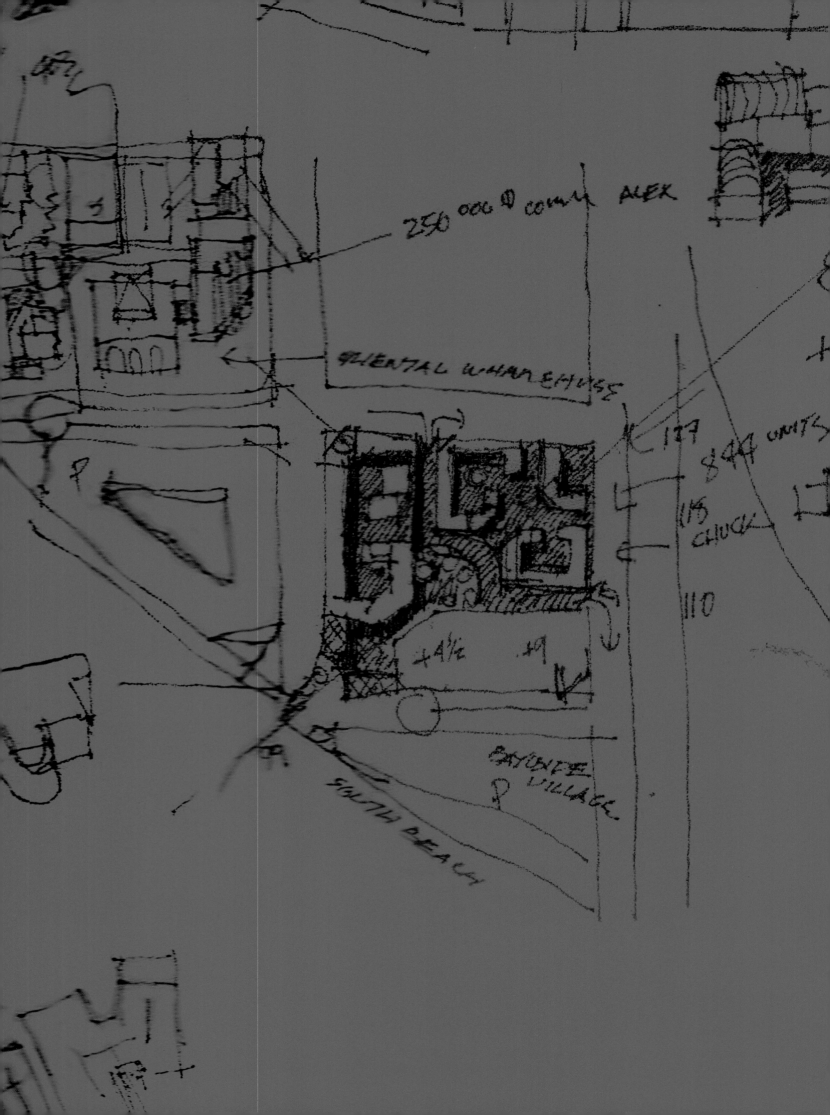

Foreword

Frank Anton

For more than forty years, when it comes to housing design, Rodney Friedman has been the irresistible force to the mainstream housing industry's immoveable object. For more than thirty of those years, first as editor of BUILDER magazine, the leading magazine for that mainstream industry, and currently as CEO of Hanley Wood, the leading publisher for the construction industry, I've had a front row seat to that battle royale. I'll have to admit that I've always been pulling for Rodney to win.

The back-and-forth battle began in the 1960s. Back then builders in California were throwing up drab tract houses as fast as they could. Rodney countered with a community of single family houses called Sunset San Marin. These affordable homes had sleek, wood exteriors and exciting, open interior spaces. No flat ceilings and undersized windows. The battle was joined.

At Whaler's Cove in Foster City, California, Rodney created real neighborhoods of simple but elegant (restrained also comes to mind as an adjective) homes when most builders were content to grind out monotonous subdivisions. As the overwhelming majority of builders continued to, in effect, endorse and defend sprawl, Rodney – almost a full generation before both his architectural peers and builders – took up the call for an alternative: an urban, high-density, mixed use development. Located in the heart of downtown San Francisco and called Golden Gateway Commons, it stretched for three blocks. Scaled perfectly and built with brick in sympathy to nearby older buildings Golden Gateway Commons set an early standard for urban infill development and proved that urban living could be a real, desirable alternative to suburban tract projects.

When, over the last ten years, the housing industry gave itself over almost exclusively to building monstrous McMansions, Rodney counterpunched with a home like the Aptekar residence in Stinson Beach, California. Yes, this is a custom home, not a production home, but at 3,500 square feet it's about half the size and half the price of many McMansions. Subtle, low slung, dominated by big glass walls, clad with a single material, the house stands in stark and proud contrast to the gawky, over-sized, over-ornamented houses that, alas, have spread across the whole country.

There are in this book many more good examples of Rodney's outstanding work, which over his distinguished career totals over 250,000 housing units. Put another way, Rodney has landed 250,000 good, hard punches to the gut and the chin of his adversaries. He's tirelessly spoken to builder audiences and lobbied magazine editors to be more selective about what they published. He's fought the good fight. But during the same time, the mainstream housing industry built more than 50 million units. So clearly in the battle royale Rodney has waged, he has been, for the most part, one against many. He's never given up, but I have seen him frustrated.

Why? Twenty years ago he told me that if you asked 100 Americans, be they doctors or plumbers or bankers or teachers or even small children, to draw a house, they'd draw a square punctured by a door and four windows, topped by a triangle with a chimney. Since then as I've traveled the country speaking to housing industry groups I've asked thousands of Americans to draw a house, and virtually every one of them has drawn the picture Rodney described. So, Rodney is frustrated sometimes because the form of a house is so simple, so iconic as to be known to even most children. Yet, the mainstream housing industry continues to try, with little success and far too often disastrous results, to improve upon a very good thing.

Rodney wishes, as do I, that that would stop. His body of work makes a strong case for that. But he did not, because he could not, single-handedly convince the mainstream of the housing industry to espouse his simple, elegant form of architectural modernism. Is he frustrated still? Probably. But, without question, his influence, particularly in California, the epicenter of the American housing industry, has been pervasive and positive. Still practicing, he continues to fight the good fight.

Introduction

John T. Friedman, FAIA

By the 1950's, the University of California at Berkeley had established one of the nation's leading architectural schools under the dean of the legendary William W. Wurster, and in the spirit of the great regionalist Bernard Maybeck. The faculty included Eric Mendlesohn, Joseph Esherick, and Ernest Born. There were visiting professors such as Buckminster Fuller, Paul Rudolph and Charles Eames. Rodney Friedman, A. Robert Fisher, and Robert Geering were students in architectural school at Berkeley at that time.

It was hard to grow up in West Los Angeles in the 1940's and not be conscious of construction. Houses were being built in profusion and the young Rodney Friedman found the process, and the unclad structures in particular, fascinating. Once he asked his mother, "Who does that?" She responded, "Architects." His career choice was sealed at age 10.

The school, and Eames and Esherick in particular, put a strong emphasis on construction, on how things actually got built, that stayed with Friedman throughout his professional career. He recalls that many of the student problems were set up so that structural considerations were interwoven and inseparable from architectural design. Friedman became Eames' teaching assistant and visited his famed home and studio in Southern California.

After graduation in 1956, Friedman joined the San Francisco office of Welton Becket and Associates, one of the largest firms on the West Coast. A. Robert Fisher, who received his Master of Architecture degree from Berkeley in 1953, was Director of Design, and Robert Geering, who had received his graduate degree in 1954, was also a designer at the Becket firm. Among the specialties of the firm were shopping centers, the largest of which was in San Francisco, built by the Stoneson family of developers. The firm also had a home building arm that was losing market share to developer Joseph Eichler. The Stoneson houses were traditional builder products while the Eichler houses had open plans, glass walls, and radiant heating, all well suited to the California climate and Californian's fondness for the outdoors.

Fisher left the Becket firm in 1962 to found his own architectural firm, and Bob Geering joined him shortly thereafter. In 1964, Friedman and A. Robert Fisher formed their partnership, Fisher-Friedman Associates, with Robert Geering as senior associate.

Among their first clients was Stoneson, for whom they designed development houses that were similar to Eichler's in openness and tall volumes but were more substantial. More attention was paid to things like kitchen cabinets and exterior walls, which were sturdier than Eichler's favored plywood. The FFA house utilized suitable construction techniques for hillsides as well as flat sites, especially significant as the supply of the latter dwindled.

The firm also designed a series of custom houses in the Bay Region mode, consciously adapting their design elements to mass housing. Its reputation among merchant builders spread and it attracted large-scale commissions such as Green Hills in Millbrae, Monte Verde in San Bruno and one of the first large scale planned unit townhouse developments of the time – Casitas Alameda in Alameda, California.

Developers were asking for higher densities and FFA moved into design of planned developments and of garden apartments, notable in three Newport Beach projects – Mariner Square, Baywood and Promontory Point. All had elements of community, including a commons at Mariner Square and a recreation center and landmark clock tower at Baywood. They also marked a departure from post and beam construction, partly influenced by the work of Charles Moore and others at the widely celebrated Sea Ranch on the Northern California Coast. While others focused upon and often imitated the Sea Ranch style, FFA was most intrigued by the structural systems of the early Sea Ranch buildings, especially the first condominium. It had a 12x12x12 foot grid of hefty structural members wrapped in a wooden skin. This technique freed the exterior walls to be punctured by all sorts of elements and allowed windows to be placed where they would most benefit the building's occupants. FFA, inspired by the freedom of Sea Ranch, used the concept less the 12x12x12 foot grid, in the Newport Beach project and thereafter.

By the mid 1970's, awards were coming to the firm from a variety of sources and its work had become a staple of both the architectural and housing press, which Friedman was skilled at cultivating. All of this

brought a widening variety of clients, which allowed the firm to explore new avenues of form. In Newport Beach, FFA designed the tile-roofed Promontory Point almost as a Mediterranean hill town. A little later the firm made the Islands at Foster City on San Francisco Bay a composition of color-accented white cubes reflected in the surrounding waters. Shingled Peter Coutts Hill housing at the Stanford University campus has a variety of punched out windows and is accented with colors reflecting the flavorful early campus buildings.

The firm's most urban work came with Golden Gateway Commons in the lap of downtown San Francisco. It is comprised of low-rise brick condominiums atop a two-story commercial podium. The residential layer, heavily landscaped, has the feeling of an elevated park. The project not only reflects the character of this cosmopolitan city but also augments it.

Across San Francisco Bay to the north in the charming town of Tiburon, the firm went beyond architecture into urban design. Its Point Tiburon project placed three condominium neighborhoods around a commercial core, with a shoreline park, bird sanctuary and fresh water lagoon.

As the 1970's turned into the 1980's, architecture, and especially development housing, was taken over by postmodernism, which Friedman characterized as a license to copy 15th century buildings. "The problem with that," he says, "is that many architects who are inspired to do this are tasteless. The quality of their work is terrible, and it's multiplying like a virus all around the world."

In addition to historicism, postmodernism is about new buildings respecting their surroundings. Hasn't this been a hallmark of FFA? Friedman responds that "architecture can be distinctive and compatible at the same time. New buildings can incorporate elements of their older neighbors, but they must declare themselves as definitely new."

Postmodernism also gave architects new freedom to experiment with form. While remaining steadfastly modern in its basic approach, FFA has made use of that freedom in recent projects such as the multi-storied graduate student apartments at the University of California at Irvine and the cellular, almost tent-like Vintage Club in Indian Wells.

The only unabashedly postmodern form in FFA's portfolio is the Pleasant Hill City Hall, and that was done in design collaboration with Charles Moore. In recent years, FFA has done a series of projects in collaboration with such distinguished architects as Moore, Cesar Pelli, Arthur Erickson and Craig Hartman. "There is never a question of credit," says Rodney Friedman. "It is always made clear who is the principal designer, as it was with Moore at Pleasant Hill. Such collaboration is beneficial in two ways; it is a learning experience and it often takes the firm into building types it hasn't done before, opening new doors into future work." Pleasant Hill for instance led directly to Redwood City City Hall and the city of Emeryville engaging FFA to do its new

city hall. The Emeryville project is a good example of FFA's brand of contextualism. The existing city hall, built in 1903, was "a quite competent replica of a small Palladian villa'" in Friedman's words, "with a dome and a colonnade." The city first asked FFA to investigate remodeling its little gem. The firms' recommendation was to keep some functions such as the council chamber in the old building, but put the municipal offices in a modernist new building next to it. "The concept was to make the new building as transparent as possible; a background building, deferential to the old historic one."

At one point, FFA's work was 90 percent residential, but now it grows more varied with each passing year and includes academic buildings, office developments, civic facilities and urban design. Still, over the years, FFA has designed or built more than 250,000 residential units with thousands more in progress. Its work has won more that 200 awards and has been published virtually everywhere.

While dean of the College of Environmental Design at the University of California at Berkeley, Roger Montgomery commended the firm for "realizing the nearly impossible goal of actually building distinguished architecture for the community development and home building industries."

A. Robert Fisher retired in 2000; Robert Geering retired from FFA in 2005; and Rodney Friedman continues in his role as chief architect and designer, leading the practice as the only original founder. Rodney Friedman has been a visiting professor and guest lecturer at some of the most prestigious architecture schools in America and Australia. He has been invited to lecture to professional organizations in America, Asia and Europe. FFA's buildings have been exhibited in the Museum of Modern Art in San Francisco and New York, and in the 1989 traveling exhibition of Soviet and American architecture.

The year 2010 will mark the tenth anniversary of Robert Fisher's retirement from FFA. Following Robert Fisher's retirement, Mark B. Steppan, AIA, CSI, NCARB, (University of California, Berkeley in 1979) has carried on the role of assisting Rodney Friedman in all major policy decisions and continues to excel in managing and directing the firm's institutional and academic projects. David Tritt, AIA (University of Pennsylvania's Graduate School of Fine Arts in 1972) assists Rodney Friedman in the execution and continuation of the firm's design goals. Nathan Ogle, AIA (Columbia University, Masters of Science in Architecture and Urban Design in 1995) has taken a major role in project management and assists with client relations. This core group of professionals carries forward as the new FFA. Rodney Friedman continues to lead FFA in the 21st century as the design force. He has been honored by the AIACC1993 *Firm Award* and the AIACC 2006 *Presidential Citation*, as well as the very first AIACC *Distinguished Practice Award* in 2007. In 2006, Rodney Friedman, FAIA was inducted into the inaugural class of the *Builder's Choice Housing Hall of Fame for Design Excellence*.

In Praise of Pragmatism

Daniel Solomon, FAIA

Rodney Friedman is an architect with a peculiar and noble narrative, one that belongs all to him, and is quite unlike the life-story that most architecture students dream of when they imagine how their career will unfold. Rodney's career has been a triumph – gratifying to him and a large contribution to the world. But it is a success of a different kind from the run-of-the-mill geniuses that most architects struggle so hard to be. That Rodney lays no particular claim to genius is in itself an impressive and especially winning achievement. Imagine an architect with a vast production of handsome, well-made buildings over a hard-working lifetime who does not consider himself a seminal form-giver. It shatters the mold.

Rodney's life story is that of a master practitioner, purveyor and custodian of a tradition he did not invent. It is a tradition of domestic architecture that has for most of its existence been the special domain of a small, privileged Northern California elite. Rodney's body of work captures the union with landscape, abundant sunlight, craftsmanship, informal ease and domestic comfort that for many decades characterized the best of Bay Region modernism. He has made these qualities accessible to many thousands of people for whom a house by Gardner Daly, William Wurster, Charles Moore or Joseph Esherick was an unattainable dream.

Far more than any of those somewhat rarified masters, Rodney is a creature of the hurly-burly of the world. Many tough and pragmatic characters who make a living developing housing for the marketplace love and trust Rodney. That is no small achievement. Where most of California's production building of mass housing has devolved to the lowest common denominator of taste and craft, the projects of Fisher-Friedman stand distinctly apart. From Rodney's smallest single houses, to scores of medium density housing complexes of distinction, to large dormitory complexes and urban high-rises, there is a consistent level of excellence and livability. It is an extraordinary exercise of intelligence, of relentless determination, of crafty pragmatism, that has allowed him to shape with elegance and care more large pieces of the world than most architects would ever touch in six lifetimes. And he isn't finished yet.

Custom Housing

Friedman Residence

Belvedere, California

The Friedman residence was designed by the architect for himself and his family on a picturesque and difficult site on the east side of Belvedere Island. Overlooking Belvedere Cove and the San Francisco Yacht Club, the site enjoys an abundance of morning sunlight. Native stands of oak, eucalyptus and pine were preserved on the site to maintain a well-established character.

The plan is compartmentalized so that the family can enjoy one another's company in shared spaces and obtain privacy in other spaces. The open rooms on the entry level are designed to be used as family meeting places and social areas. The lower level contains the master bedroom suite which includes a sitting area approximately 18 feet square. Two children's rooms, a second bathroom and a laundry room are also on this level. Every room enjoys a view either to the south or east.

The home is designed as a system of walls penetrated in designated places to maximize light and views. Because of the steep grade of the site, the large deck on the east side is supported by tie rods thus eliminating the need for long columns and supports. Numerous skylights and a greenhouse are placed to take advantage of the sun and light as well as extensive panoramic views of Tiburon, Angel Island and San Francisco Bay.

Vertical 1x6-inch redwood boards treated with clear water sealer were utilized as the basic exterior material with dark anodized aluminum trim on windows and skylights. Black painted metal trim and a copper roof complete the limited package of exterior materials. Interior materials are limited to white painted sheet rock walls, dark stained hardwood floors and three-inch square dark blue ceramic tile by Heath.

A successful contrast between the dark and weathering exterior with the light and spacious interior gives this home a unique character that makes it a distinctive addition to its surroundings. Since its completion in 1972, the house has weathered gracefully.

Below Living room, Dining room
Left East elevation

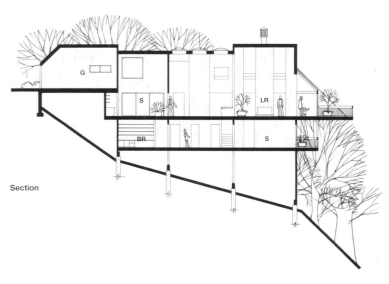

Section

Far Left Living room looking towards library
Upper Right Living Room looking east
Lower Right Kitchen looking towards studio

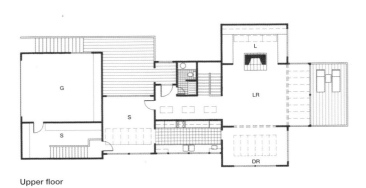

Upper floor

Lower floor

Seiger Residence

Los Altos Hills, California

The Seiger residence is located in the rolling countryside of the San Francisco Peninsula on a gently sloping acre of land with a small creek at the bottom of the slope. The house is sited parallel to the slope and is dug slightly into the slope along its longitudinal direction.

The home is composed of four simple rectilinear forms and has a mixture of shed and flat roofs. The house and carport are sheathed with shingles; doors and windows are framed in wood with a natural finish. The west side, oriented to the downhill and more scenic view, features a structured vine-covered arbor set out from the west wall of the house to screen the late afternoon sun and provide a pleasantly shaded outdoor living space.

One approaches the entrance on the east side by walking along a path between the side of the house and a low vine covered retaining wall. Arriving at the front door, located at the midpoint of the house, one enters a generous reception area opening to a view of the grass covered hills to the west. The reception area separates the residence into two zones – family and adult. To the right on the entry level is the living room. The master bedroom suite is above on the second level. To the left of the reception area is the dining room and spacious kitchen with a light airy breakfast area set in a greenhouse. Two children's bedrooms and a play loft are located above this area.

Left West elevation
Below North elevation

Above Family room
Right Living Room

Section

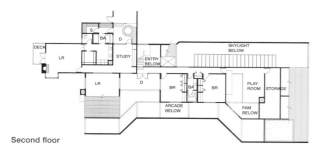

Second floor

First floor

Aptekar Residence

Stinson Beach, California

This distinctive beachfront residence required special considerations to address restrictive FEMA requirements, local jurisdictional height restrictions, storm surge from the sea and the necessary selection of materials resistant to damage from salt air.

An L-shaped plan allows ocean views from anywhere within the "Grand Salon" living room with open kitchen and the master bedroom, while giving privacy to the guest rooms and study. At the entrance on the street side, a ship-type ramp rises to the living level set eleven feet above sea level (to satisfy FEMA requirements). Inside, the nautical theme of a sailing vessel is enhanced by the use of exposed and oversized varnished wood columns to support the roof. Stainless steel tie rods spanning the vaulted cedar ceiling evoke images of ship's rigging.

Left and Below West elevation

Opening from the "Grand Salon" on the ocean side, a glass enclosed deck spans the width of the house and provides shelter from seasonal winds and temperature fluctuations. An open stairway leads from the elevated deck to the beach.

The house is clad in white cedar shingles, roofed with a standing seam copper roofing system.

Above Living room "Grand Salon"
Below Kitchen porch
Right Kitchen

Following Pages West elevation

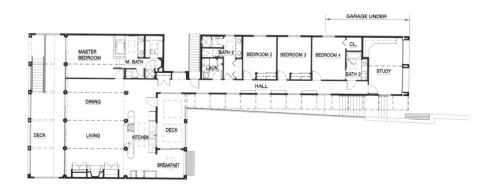

Floor plan

Single-Family Detached Merchant Built Homes

Sunset San Marin

Novato, California

Sunset San Marin is an innovative subdivision project designed by FFA in the early 60's. Located in Novato, California the site covers approximately 100 acres and was subdivided to provide lots for moderately priced, individual, mass produced single family residences.

Two model plans were designed. The larger house contains 1,750 square feet of interior living space on a site of approximately 7,500 square feet. The smaller house, on about the same size lot, contains 1,300 square feet.

Each of the houses can have three different exteriors while utilizing the same basic floor plan. Changes also alter both roof lines and exterior surfaces. The purpose is to minimize the usual sub-division look-alike problem. Further variation is achieved by reversing the floor plan; each house works equally well in a left or right model.

The floor plans of both houses are similar. The kitchen is the central element and divides the family room from the living-dining areas. It is open, but can be closed off. The hooklike projection of the kitchen wall into the living room serves to define dining space.

Each master bedroom has its own dressing room and bath.

The houses seem even more spacious than they actually are due in part to the use of lofty ceilings and floor to ceiling glass. Each major room uses floor-to-ceiling glass to open up to the outside, allowing sheltered private garden courts, secure children's play areas, etc. These protected exterior spaces really are outdoor extensions of the floor plans, utilizing a kind of "full lot floor-planning". Both houses have covered entry walks, imparting an arbor or trellis-like approach to the house.

Left and Below Rear elevations

Whaler's Cove

Foster City, California

Whaler's Cove consists of two interconnected parcels, *Whaler's Landing* on the shore, and *Whaler's Isle*. All dwelling units are detached single-family houses. On the *Isle* all of the homes are oriented to the water, as are most of the homes on the *Landing.* Many previous schemes for this site were inward oriented, whereas the intent of FFA's plan was to exploit the water orientation as much as possible.

Both the *Isle* and *Landing* are laid out in a series of cul-de-sac streets. The *Isle* cul-de-sacs alternate with inlets cut into the island by the architects to bring the lagoon into the center of the property, eliminating through traffic.

All dwellings are basically "through-type" plans with the living areas at the rear facing the water. On the *Landing* they are zero lot line houses. The upper story in the A and B models is tucked up under the roof, opening the side yard to light and space. This traditional American housing type was particularly inspired by Wright's early studio in Oak Park.

On the *Isle*, the houses are larger and detached on all sides forming the lot line. The A unit is one story with a sky lit atrium; the B unit is a two-story salt box; the C unit is another quasi-bungalow similar to the A and B models of the Landing.

The buildings are finished in the either cedar shingles or vertical resawn boards, both with a naturally weathered finish. Limited to doors, windows, and gutters, colors are limited. The colors and materials are used in various combinations to create variety.

Left Waterfront elevation
Below Aerial view

Upper Left Aerial view
Lower Left Waterfront elevation
Above Living room

First floor

Second Floor

Marin View

Marin County, California

A 300-acre parcel of extremely difficult terrain located in the coastal hills between Mill Valley and Sausalito is the site for this development of single family detached dwellings. Because the average slope of the site is in excess of 3 to 1, the roadways were planned first so as to save the virgin timber and ground cover; the remaining land was used for home sites. A full 50 per cent of the site has been deeded to the county of Marin for a trails and park system. The homes are designed to reflect the rural character of the site with the juxtaposition of roofs and geometry producing a citadel-like quality on the wooded foothills.

The houses are designed to be sited on steep downhill lots and are unusual in their use of space and volume. One enters the home by crossing a bridge to the front door, entering the residence on a mid level landing between the master bedroom suite on an upper level and the living room with a sunken inglenook, dining room, kitchen, and family room below. The children's bedroom area, additional bath and storage rooms are on another level below the family spaces, separating the adult and junior members of the family. High ceilings and interesting volumes play a great part in emphasizing the kind of environment produced by the plan.

All the foundations consist of drilled piers and grade beams with conventional frame construction above. The project was completed in 1972.

Re-sawn Douglas Fir plywood stained in harmony with earth tones is employed on all exteriors. The roofs are a combination of cedar shingles and tar and gravel. All the glazing is aluminum and anodized a medium bronze. Metal chimneys add to the mountain like character of the homes. The project is extremely successful in terms of sales and proves that developers can develop hillsides gracefully and successfully.

Left East elevation
Below North elevation

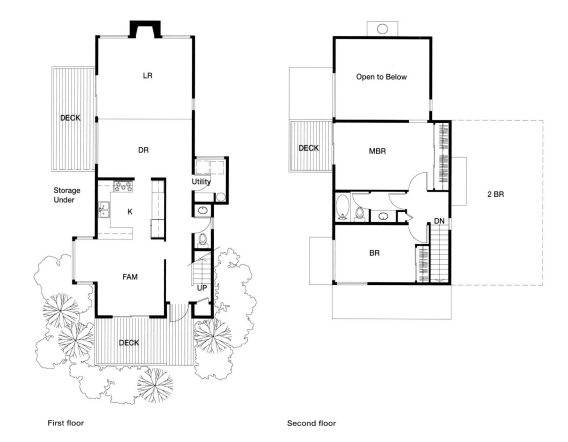

First floor   Second floor

Left South elevation
Below East elevation

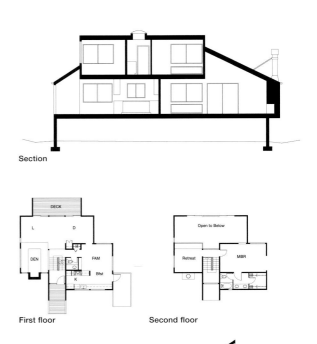

Section

DECK

L   D

DEN   FAM

K   Bfst

First floor

Open to Below

Retreat   MBR

Second floor

BR   BR

Storage   Unexcavated

Basement

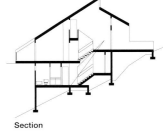

Section

Right Aerial looking west
Above Fireplace
Below Kitchen

Sonoma House I and II

Sonoma, California

The developer for these homes was a first time developer and his business partner—a general contractor, who built the houses. An existing 3/4-acre parcel was divided into three parts, the largest containing the owner/developers existing home and the remainder subdivided into two parcels of about 7,700 square feet each. The original intent was for the design to be in a traditional or southwest style; but the developers were later persuaded that a market for modern housing in spec development existed and agreed to the design of two distinctly different Modern styles.

House I, the corner house, was designed as a simple rectilinear modern plaster finished dwelling. Because of large setbacks on three sides and planning requirements that changed late in the design process the floor plan became a straightforward T shape, two stories high, with a detached garage.

House II is conceptually a single-vault roof shape mass, cut in two and splayed apart, opening to the rear of the property. The two wings are connected by a link, lower in height; almost all glass on the private rear side and mostly solid on the street side. The exterior is clad in eastern white cedar shingles.

Both houses have large aluminum widows, volume ceilings over living rooms, lofts, and separate bathrooms for each bedroom. The well equipped kitchens are both open to and share space with a family room that opens to the rear yard.

Costs for these houses were kept under control. They sold for approximately $1.5 million each. One of the most distinguishing aspects of this project was the ability of the modern design of the homes to appeal to buyers looking for a more traditional style.

The houses were designed by Mark B. Steppan, AIA, CSI, NCARB, of FFA; and Alison Friedman Steppan.

Left North elevation
Below South elevation

Above and Far Right West elevation

First floor

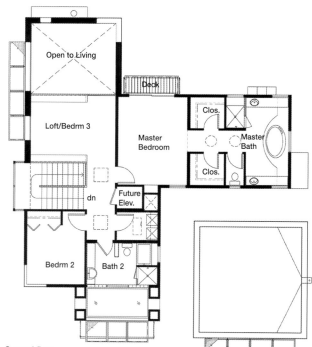

Second floor

Second floor

First floor

Above South elevation House II
Below Kitchen House II
Opposite upper right Living room House I
Opposite upper left and below Stairs and bridges House II

Duplexes and Townhouses

Strawberry Hill Duplexes

Marin County, California

Strawberry Hill is a community of 52 single-family zero lot line duplexes located just off Highway 101 in Marin County, minutes away from downtown San Francisco. The project was designed for a market of middle income empty-nesters and young families with one or two children. The project was also directed at people working and living in San Francisco who wanted to move out of the city as well as to those living in northern Marin County wishing to relocate closer to urban workplaces.

The Strawberry site has an unusual constraint due to its particular hillside location. There are units that face south to a beautiful panoramic view of San Francisco, while those to the north look toward Mount Tamalpais and overlook the busy freeway. The units facing the city sold rapidly, whereas the dwellings facing the Highway were slower to sell. To compensate for the two different locations, pricing and sale phasing were adjusted to make for an equal absorption of both unit types.

Another unique feature of this project is that it had existing approval for a high density 180-unit three story parking condominium project requiring massive grading. After this type of building was deemed inappropriate for the site, FFA's subsequent redesign accomplished the reduction of grading, use of the natural hillside, minimization of density, and optimum exposure to the views. The redesign resulted in the creation of 26 zero lot line duplexes. The zero lot line concept created the impression that two units were actually a single family detached house.

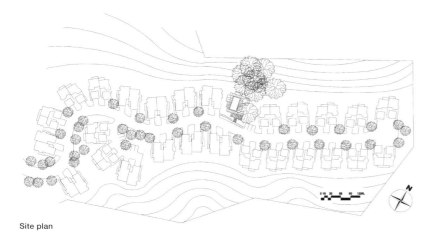

Site plan

Left East elevation
Below Looking south

Second floor

Third floor

Second floor

First floor

Plan A

Lower floor

Third Floor

First Floor

Second Floor

Plan B

Plan C

Turtle Rock Glen Townhouses

Irvine, California

Site plan

This 50-unit cluster project is situated on two exposed knolls in Orange County overlooking a broad plain of housing and agricultural land to the west. At the request of the client, FFA designed a cluster project that could be situated in various locations on the ranch. The specific locations are composed of small rounded hills that occur at random on the property. Instead of flattening the hills, a concept was developed whereby a cluster of well-designed townhouses could be arranged in nodes and sited on these hilltops to complement the natural terrain and avoid further impact on the landscape. Turtle Rock Glen is built on two such small hills with 22 units on one hill and 28 units on the other. The hills are connected by a lushly landscaped greenbelt that also includes a recreation center providing swimming and tennis facilities. Landscaping with broad lawns and numerous deciduous trees completes the residential enclave.

The nodes are composed of five floorplans varying in size from 1,400 square feet to 1,750 square feet. They are composed of townhouses with attached garages and tri-level townhouses with parking close by. All units have raised ceilings with an abundance of glass and skylights, commodious master bedrooms and baths, generous decks, and strong view orientation. The limited palette of exterior materials includes resawn cedar siding stained in earth tones, cedar shingle roofs, dark anodized aluminum window frames, blue painted gutters and bright blue Sunbrella awnings.

Left and Below View from common green

Left Entry at motor court
Above Aerial view

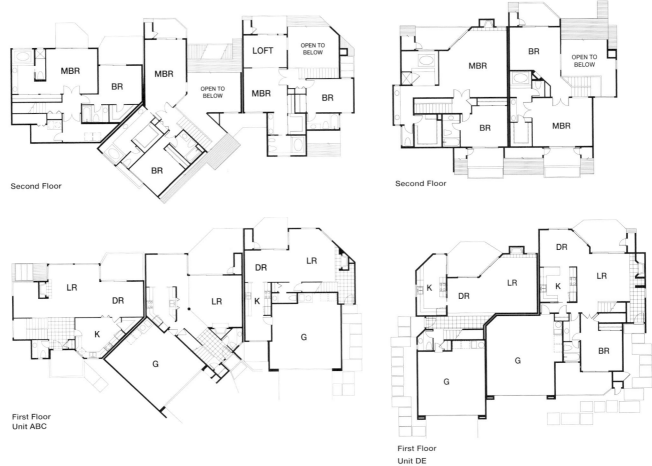

Second Floor

Second Floor

First Floor
Unit ABC

First Floor
Unit DE

Ocean Point Townhouses

Pacifica, California

Ocean Point is located just south of San Francisco on a sloped 10-acre parcel facing the Pacific Ocean and bordered by a natural hillside preserve. The primary siting consideration was to maintain minimal interference with the ocean views of existing homes on Beachview Avenue. The townhouses were kept at two stories with low roof levels and were situated on the site to provide view corridors. Each of the two or three-bedroom units, ranging from 1,480 to 1,640 square feet, has a glass-enclosed front patio adjoining an upper-story living room from which the ocean view can be enjoyed in the prevailing cool and windy climate. Other design features include rear patios, two-story foyers, skylights, fireplaces and two-car garages arranged in motor courts. Some townhouses have passive solar greenhouses. Residents have access to a pool house which includes an indoor-outdoor swimming pool and an indoor Jacuzzi.

Cedar shingles were selected as the exterior material. A red-rock color was selected for the roofs to complete the palette of materials.

Left Looking east

Site plan

LOFT | Open to Below

Second Floor

Unit A
First Floor

K | BA
DR | LR | BR

Unit B

BA | BR
K
DR | LR

Unit C
First Floor

MBR
B | B
BR

Second Floor

LR
DR
K
B
FR

Unit D
First Floor

BR | MBR
B
BR

Second Floor

LR
S
K | DR
FR | B

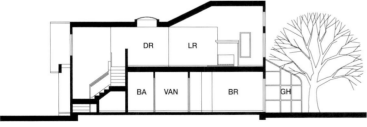

Section

Left Pool house
Above Looking southeast
Right Pool house interior

The Islands

Foster City, California

The site of this condominium project is a pair of islands, the focal point of a large lagoon near San Francisco Bay. The main approach road to Foster City is on the opposite shore.

The geometrical shapes of the buildings, as well as the use of white exteriors complemented by bright yellow awnings and blue tile roofs, read strongly from across the lagoon, both as an outline against the sky and as a reflection on the water.

There are two similar building types in the project. The ground floor consists of two flats (identical in both buildings) facing the water, with garages fronting the street. The upper floor consists of a pair of two-story townhouses in the middle of a one-story townhouse on each end. The upper units have high ceilings and double story living rooms. Most of the middle units have family rooms with a greenhouse extension overlooking the street. Many units have balconies.

On the smaller of the two islands 6-unit buildings comprise the first phase of the project and all are located facing the water along both sides and at each end of the island. Circulation for both automobiles and pedestrians is provided by an internal street which branches off in both directions from the entry turnaround.

Each island has a clubhouse. Sited on the water's edge and extending into the water like the bow of a boat the clubhouse on the smaller island conveys a nautical theme. Two stories high with volume ceilings and a prominent signature tower, the clubhouse overlooks the pool, Jacuzzi and outdoor areas. It is intentionally sited off-axis to preserve a view to the lagoon. In the center of the larger island, a second horseshoe shaped clubhouse is set into the land in order to maximize views for the neighboring dwellings.

Left Clubhouse

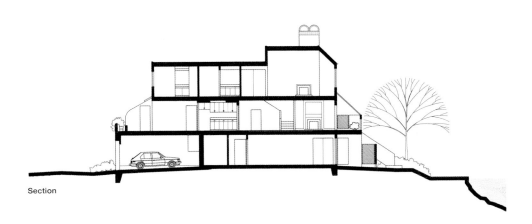

Section

Left Looking north
Upper Right Aerial view
Lower Right Pool house

Following Pages
Left Aerial View
Right Drive

Above Clubhouse interior
Far Right Pool house interior

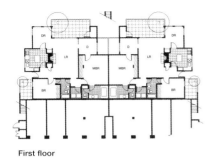

First floor

Second floor

Third floor

Shorebirds Solar Village

Redwood City, California

Shorebird Solar Village is a water-oriented community, with most of the units sited on either a natural saltwater lagoon or an interior lake. All units are designed to maximize a variety of views, from the intimacy of the lake to the distant views of the lagoon.

At the project's main entry a recreation center features a large sky-lit lounge, fireplace and kitchen. A loft connects the recreation center to a solar heated swimming pool, Jacuzzi and thermal pool located near the lagoon. At the southern end of the site a second pool and recreation facility is also located along the lagoon.

Two and three-bedroom condominium townhouses and flats comprise the 172 units. Ground floor dwellings have 9-foot high ceilings and outdoor patios; the upper level dwellings have cathedral ceilings and decks. Many of the upper flats also have lofts overlooking the living areas.

Some residents park in one or two-car garages with direct access to the dwellings; others park in secured garages tucked under buildings. Residents walk to their units through landscaped courtyards and up private stairs to reach second level homes.

With energy efficiency as a main feature of the project, domestic hot water and water for the swimming pools is solar heated. Solar panels are located on flat portions of the roofs. All doors and windows are double-glazed. The buildings are fully insulated. On selected units with southern exposure, passive solar greenhouses help to conserve energy and extend living space.

Exteriors are finished in white stucco, plum-colored glazed flat tile roofs and matching trim accented by blue awnings to evoke the feeling of a coastal Mediterranean village.

Left Looking north
Below Looking south

Above Entry
Right Aerial looking north

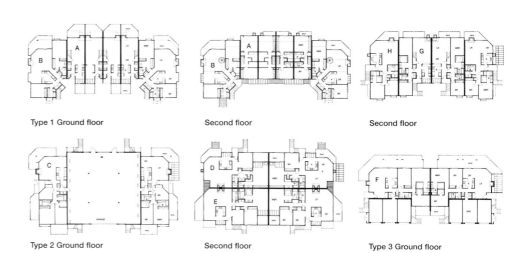

Type 1 Ground floor

Second floor

Second floor

Type 2 Ground floor

Second floor

Type 3 Ground floor

Harbortown

San Mateo, California

Harbortown is an irregular shaped parcel of 28 acres of reclaimed bay wetlands bounded by city streets on one side and a lagoon on the other. The primary aim of the site plan is to provide maximum water orientation to all dwellings.

Over half the units look out upon the Marina Lagoon whose shoreline is bordered by a specially designed promenade accessing boat docking facilities which are set at a lower elevation to avoid conflict with resident's privacy and views. The remaining dwellings are arranged around a man-made interior lagoon.

The residences are composed in two basic configurations; some in rows and others arranged in 12-unit clusters. The interior of the clusters contain a motor court with six garages on each side and a pedestrian courtyard in the rear. Entrances to most of the units are off this court, with the entrance to the remainder from green spaces between the clusters. Unit types consist of flats and townhouses.

Recreation facilities include tennis courts, boat storage facilities, tot lots and two pool complexes. The main complex has both a large outdoor pool and an indoor pool. The secondary swimming pool has a smaller recreation building.

Sheathed in horizontal boards or shingles, the buildings present an irregular, randomly ordered appearance reminiscent of coastal New England villages. They are set at angles to each other to best utilize an irregular site and to create an interesting and varied edge along the shore.

Left View from waterfront
Below Aerial looking south

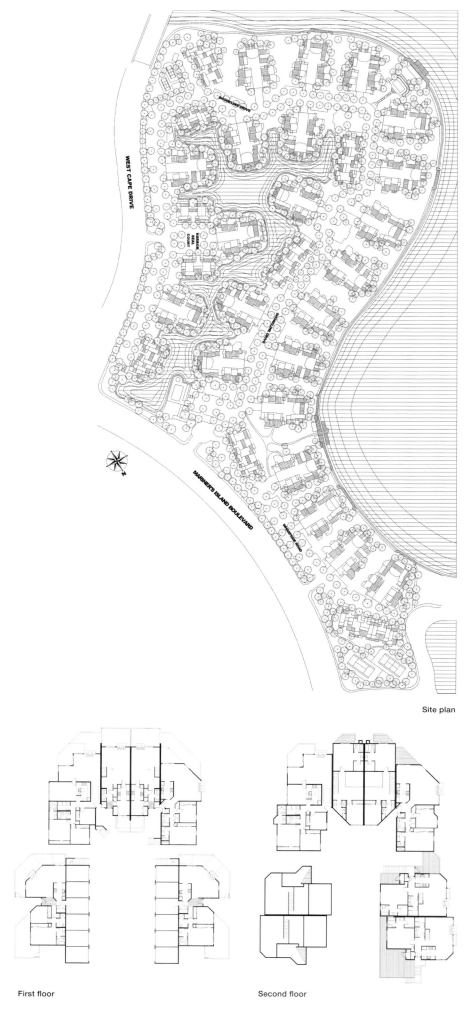

Site plan

First floor

Second floor

Right Living room

Lighthouse Cove

Redwood Shores, California

Lighthouse Cove is a 124-unit condominium project located on a secluded site on San Francisco Bay. The buildings along the outer lagoon have been designed to take maximum advantage of the water orientation. In order to provide all the inner units with a comparable water view, an interior water system was created. As a result, all but two of the condominiums have water frontage.

All the buildings are sheathed in cedar shingles which have weathered to a soft, silvery tone. The forms of the structures recall the Shingle Style buildings of coastal New England, employing a dormer and arched window theme throughout. The volumetric quality of the buildings is emphasized by the unity of roof and wall materials, minimal trim, and simple cut-out window openings.

There are three basic unit types at Lighthouse Cove, ranging in size from 811 to 1,359 square feet. Two units are townhouses and the third is a flat. The townhouse unit fits into the central part of the typical building configuration, allowing the footprint to be longer or shorter depending on the location. The end unit is always flat, permitting the building to wrap around corners or to make a transition to an adjacent building.

Recreational facilities include a clubhouse with a lounge and kitchen and adjacent swimming pool. Boating and boat storage are also provided by the main lagoon.

Left Clubhouse
Below Aerial looking south

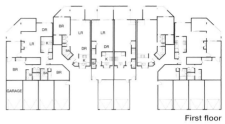

First floor

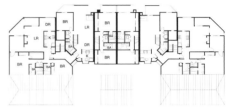

Second floor

Above View from lagoon to clubhouse
Below View from clubhouse
Right West elevation

Site plan

Half Moon Bay Condominiums

Croton-on-Hudson, New York

The Half Moon Bay Condominiums are located on 26 acres of waterfront property along the widest part of the Hudson River at Croton-on-Hudson, New York, only one hour from Manhattan. This Westchester County project is a bustling and attractive village-like community whose architecture is reminiscent of turn-of-the-century traditional architecture of the eastern seaboard.

Comprised of mostly one and one-half and two bedroom with den and loft units, the two-story wood shingled buildings are oriented toward either the Hudson River or an inland lagoon. Each unit has a view of one of the bodies of water from a private patio or deck. Half Moon Bay Condominiums are made up of 24

buildings with a total of 342 dwellings. Parking for the condominiums is provided in garages arranged in motor courts.

Included in the project is a 300-boat marina with a harbor master, a restaurant, tennis courts and a clubhouse. The clubhouse has all the qualities of a yacht club with indoor and outdoor seating, a cocktail lounge, and a full service kitchen facility. The location and design of the clubhouse allows members to enjoy a panoramic view of the Hudson River. A public gazebo with access from a community park is also included in the project with a boardwalk open to the public running the length of the property along the waterfront.

Site plan

Left Yacht club
Below Looking west

Floor Plans   First & Second Floor   First   Second   First

First Floor Plans   First   First   Second   First   Second

Below Yacht club
Right View from common green

Low-Rise Apartments

Baywood Apartments

Newport Beach, California

Baywood is a 320-unit apartment project located on the Irvine Ranch in Newport Beach, California. Units range from 790 to 1325 square feet and provide housing for families, adults, and singles. A natural swale and a deep gully running through the property provide a natural separation between the townhouses for adults and the family units.

The recreation building, featuring a signature 60-foot high clock tower, was designed as the nucleus for the community and is located at the end of a long entry drive. This building acts as a connection for the two residential areas, with a bridge from the building crossing the swale providing access to and from the adult portions of the community. Due to the very narrow size of the lot, the recreation building is lineal and uncomplicated. The building enjoys interplay of volumes; a card room overlooks the lounge area and the billiard room looks out onto the bridge and natural landscaping below. A full leasing office and laundry facilities are also located here.

The outdoor recreation area includes a regulation size Amateur Athletic Union swimming pool, lounging deck and barbecue pit. A satellite recreation space with a pool, spa, and lounging deck is provided in the adult living area.

A nursery school is located at the northeast portion of the property, connected by a series of walks to the adjacent family dwellings. A park surrounds the project on three sides. Two sides of the park are heavily forested while a deep gully on the northern boundary and a small creek preserve a natural state.

SCALE IN FEET

Site plan

Far Left Clubhouse
Above Site plan
Lower Left View from bridge
Lower Right View from clubhouse

Far Left View from common green
Upper Left Card room
Upper Right Looking east
Lower Left View from clubhouse
Lower right Aerial view

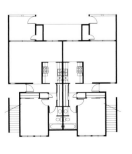

First & second floor

First & second floor

First & second floor

93

Indian Creek

Redwood City, California

Unit A

Unit B

Unit C

Unit D

Unit E

Unit F

This ten-acre site overlooking a wetlands area at the western edge of the San Francisco Bay was one of the last undeveloped parcels in the Redwood Shores mixed-use planned community. The site design solution responds to its park-like frontage on Marine Parkway, the quiet outlook over the levee, and distant views of San Francisco and the San Bruno Mountains. By facing the dwellings outward and clustering parking between the buildings, the plan takes the greatest advantage of the views. Automobile access from two points divides the site into two villages, while a continuous greenbelt connects the perimeter open space to the central recreation/leasing building and pool area. The recreation building also has visibility and access from the parkway.

The program called for upscale rental apartments within the predominantly single-family and condominium community. There are 185 apartments ranging from 680 square feet one-bedroom units to 1,030 square feet dual master bedroom units which are grouped in buildings of two and three stories. Most units have fireplaces. Upper floor apartments feature 12-foot high living room ceilings.

Due to cold prevailing breezes from the bay, a glass enclosed pool structure was designed to extend seasonal use. The enclosure can be partially opened with glazed roll-up doors. Operable ridge vents provide ventilation. A sauna, steam room, exercise space, and an aerobics room are also provided in the recreation center.

Left View from marsh
Below Looking north

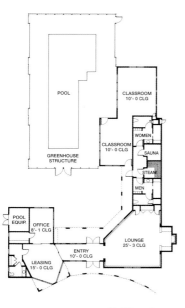

First floor plan

* **Left** Pool building looking south
* **Left** Indoor/outdoor pool
* **Right** Aerial view of entrance
* Aerial view

Park Place City Centre

Mountain View, California

Park Place is the residential portion of a major 10.69-acre mixed-use development situated in the heart of downtown Mountain View. Constructed on 7.43 acres, the complex includes four three-story, gabled wood-exterior buildings housing 370 units that are built on a podium. Parking for 700 cars is beneath the podium. One, two and three bedroom units range in size from 650 to 1,000 square feet and feature high ceilings, full-amenity kitchens, built-in fireplaces and an abundance of natural light. The architecture emphasizes courtyard living with decks and patios allowing enjoyment of the views and extensive landscaping with walkways and fountains. The project includes a recreation center, pool, spa and fitness center. Stoops were included in the design to gracefully make the transition from the podium unit to the adjoining grade.

The adjacent 3.26-acre City Centre development contains two five-story office buildings totaling 200,000 square feet of retail space on the first floors of each building and parking for 600 cars. Coupled with the nearby City Hall and Center for Performing Arts, the Park Place Centre project has helped to revitalize the historic district of Mountain View by adding convenient shops, offices and affordable housing.

Left Entry
Below Clubhouse

Upper Left Aerial looking west
Center Left Roundabout
Center Right Typical cluster
Lower Left South elevation
Lower Right Looking west
Far Right Clubhouse interior

Student and Family Housing

Graduate Student Apartments

University of California Irvine

Irvine, California

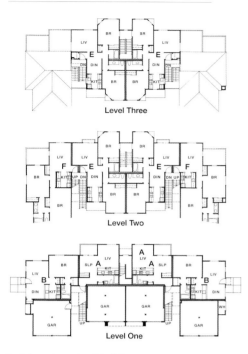

Level Three

Level Two

Level One

Left Laundry and mail building
Below Aerial view

Designed as part of an effort to attract high caliber graduate students to a campus with a dearth of affordable housing, this apartment project straddles a line which often separates student housing from market-driven apartment design.

The nine and one-half acre site is divided into two villages, each with separate automobile access. Due to the site location on the highly visible perimeter of the campus, parking is clustered within the villages with a ratio of one garage space per apartment. A recreation building, laundry facilities, and mailboxes form another cluster around a "town plaza" facing the common green between the two villages.

Student interviews and participation led to a program of studios, one bedroom one bath units, two-bedroom one-bath units and three bedroom two bath units. Arranged in buildings of 10 and 11 units, with stepping profiles of two, three, and four stories, the staggered silhouettes on the gently sloping site create a visual richness which belies the simplicity enforced by the university budget.

The complex takes on the character of a Tuscan hill town, an atmosphere reinforced by the umber and ochre color variations of the stucco exterior as well as the hipped and pyramidal shaped roofs. Detail elements are spare and become a color-coded kit of parts, featuring contrasting blue sunshades and balconies, green doors, and other accents.

Above View from common green
Lower Left Aerial of laundry and mail building
Lower Right View from parking area
Far Right Aerial

Manzanita Park II & Dining Facility

Stanford University

Palo Alto, California

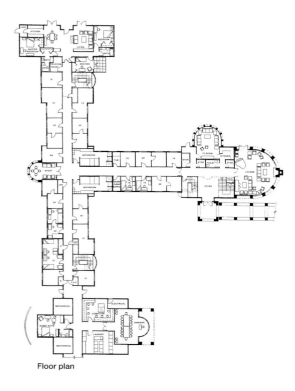

Floor plan

The Manzanita Park II and Dining Facility complex included site planning, programming, architecture and interior design services for a new undergraduate student dormitory complex to house 200 students. Located adjacent to Kimball Hall, the complex is situated at the major intersection of Campus Drive and Serra Street on the Stanford University campus. The finished building blends easily into the existing campus.

Conceptual design for Manzanita II began with a 2-day design workshop at the architect's office which resulted in a synthesis of the interests, concerns and issues raised and addressed by various campus administrative and user groups. In less than one week a scheme was prepared, overall consensus was reached and a foam model of the proposed project was assembled.

The resulting 60,000 square feet, three-story building was designed in a style to conform to the historic structures on the Stanford campus. The residence hall includes seminar, computer and study rooms as well as several lounge areas.

The incorporation of a new 20,000 square feet dining room and kitchen connected to the adjacent Kimball Hall Dining Commons was completed on schedule and occupied by students in the fall of 1992.

Far Left Aerial looking toward dining commons
Below Looking east

Following pages
Far Left Student lounge
Upper Left Aerial of quad
Upper Right Looking north
Below Study room

University Village

University of California Berkeley

Albany, California

University Village is a student family housing community located on 62 acres of land in Albany, just three miles northwest of the University of California Berkeley campus. The existing housing, built during World War II had long been scheduled by the university for replacement. In 2001, a competition was held for architects to compete for the $39 million dollar project.

FFA was selected, with Davis & Joyce Architects as associates, to design the master plan for eventual development of the entire 920 units and the detailed plans, both architectural and logistical, for the first phase of 390 units. The design goal was to provide a new residential community for families with a maximum sense of individuality.

The Village consists of smaller neighborhoods of cluster housing in the range of 30 to 45 dwellings which alternate with parking areas. Each cluster is focused around a courtyard. A large archway serves as the public entrance for each cluster. Each unit has a private front door, including the townhouse units above the flats. Each unit also has a rear access to the courtyard which provides protected space for children's play and neighborhood interaction as well as laundry and mail facilities

Floor plans of the dwellings place a strong emphasis on a family lifestyle.

A system of public open spaces and linear pathways allows the residents to move through the village by biking or walking. The network of greenways connects the open spaces and courtyards with the main pathway system. Three major greenways link all the neighborhoods to the new Village Green, the existing Village Commons and to a future city park.

The design of the streets is similar to a village, with parallel parking, street trees and entrances facing the street.

Phase I of the Village, allowing for the construction of 390 units, began in 1998, with the first group of apartments occupied in the fall of 1999.

Left Aerial View
Below North elevation

Following Pages Aerial looking north

3RD FLOOR

2ND FLOOR

1ST FLOOR

Above Entry
Far Right Courtyard and laundry building

Peter Coutts Hill

Faculty Condominiums

Stanford University, Palo Alto, California

This hillside housing community for the faculty and staff of Stanford University is located on a 20-acre hillside view site within walking distance of the central campus. Buildings, which step up and down the hillside, are compactly organized on the site, leaving 4.3 acres of hilltop space with commanding views. The 140 cedar shingled condominiums, ranging in size from 1,260 to 2,000 square feet, are grouped in clusters around a loop road.

The building clusters consist of 10 to 12 townhouses and stacked flats combined to form a "U" shape around a courtyard. Entrance to the dwellings is through these stepped courtyards along lush landscaping and past private screened patios, contributing to the creation of a smaller scale community within the project. A variety of floor plans include one, two and three-bedroom units, most of which include a study. Each unit features a garage, a private entrance, a fireplace, built-in shelving, volume ceilings and a private deck or patio.

Surrounding the building clusters are lawns and meandering paths that lead to the central recreation building located atop a knoll. The bermed recreation building is passive solar oriented and topped by a sundeck with panoramic views of the campus, foothills, and San Francisco Bay.

Left Looking north
Below Courtyard

Above Looking east
Right Aerial looking north

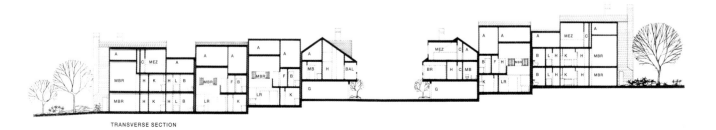

TRANSVERSE SECTION

Tercero Student Housing

University of California Davis

Davis, California

Located within the UC Davis loop road, the Tercero Housing Infill project is the first phase of a 1200 bed residential development outlined in the UCD Long Range Development Plan. FFA was commissioned to write a "Detailed Project Program" which was refined for Phase I. Phase II of the Tercero Housing Infill project consisted of two four-story buildings totally approximately 113,000 square feet.

Each building is four stories in height and is organized to contain five major levels of defensible space as a system of building community: double occupancy bedrooms, clusters of eight students (four double occupancy bedrooms), floor communities of 40-54 students with a residential advisor on each floor, building communities of 206 students and project communities of 412 students.

The dorms are served by an adjacent dining commons. To control public access, there is one locked entrance door for each 206-bed building. Circulation systems are enclosed within the interior of the building. The floor communities have been designed in such a way as to promote interaction, community, and ownership of the facility as well as to allow resident advisors to have visual and social contact with their assigned student communities.

Left and Above Entry
Below Student quad

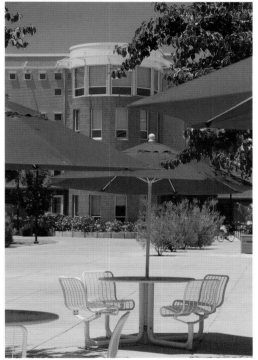

Far Left View from Dairy Road
Left Above Turrets
Left Center and Below View
from dining commons

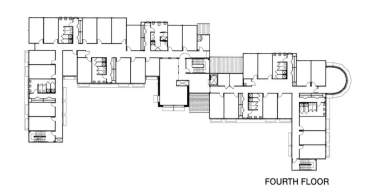

FOURTH FLOOR

INTERMEDIATE FLOORS

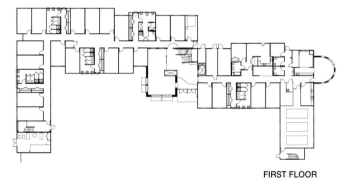

FIRST FLOOR

Upper Left Sunscreens
Upper Right Aerial view of the quad
Center Right Looking south
Bottom View from dining commons
Far Right View of turret at south building

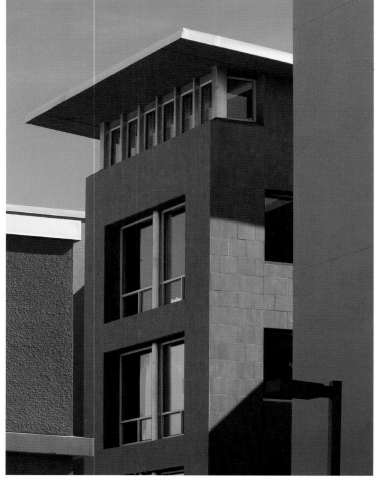

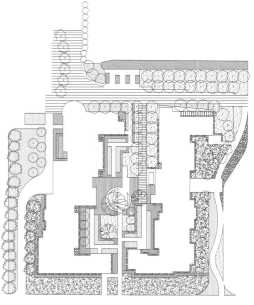

Site plan

Residential College

Houston Baptist University

Houston, Texas

At Houston Baptist University's new Student Dorms/Suites and Faculty Apartment project FFA (Design Architect) collaborated with the Houston branch of Gensler Architects (Executive Architect) to design a living/learning style higher education facility that is the prototype for future housing at this campus.

The project design, integrating an arcing building layout with an oval pond water feature, is both a benchmark component of the University's long range master plan and Phase I of the Lakes District campus plan. Use of brick, columns, outdoor terraces and water features reinforces the campus vernacular. The inclusion of a chapel supports the University's Christian faith commitment.

The 318-bed building combines 95 units with amenities that include classrooms, study rooms, a chapel, parlors, lounges and terraces, a snack bar, activity lounge and laundry facility. This Design Build project was completed in 2008.

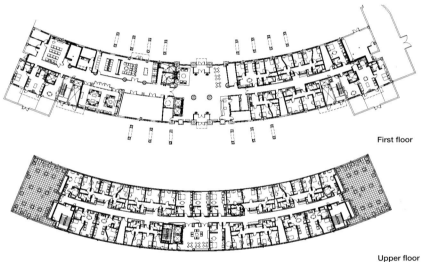

First floor

Upper floor

Left South elevation
Below Looking south

Far Left South entrance
Upper Left South elevation
Upper Right Lobby
Upper Center Hallway
Below South elevation

UCSF Mission Bay Graduate Student Housing

University of California San Francisco

San Francisco, California

This new mixed used housing complex provides 431 apartments for approximately 753 students and post-doctoral scholars (single and families). The facility offers an assortment of studios, one, two, three and four-bedroom units in four buildings. Additionally, the complex includes over 10,000 square feet of retail space and over 42,000 square feet of public and private landscaped courtyards. Offering magnificent views of the city and the bay, the site is located at the main plaza entrance on the east edge of the new UCSF Mission Bay campus on Third Street.

The project consists of four buildings arranged around a central garden courtyard that is divided between public and private spaces. The unified group of buildings hold an important position as a campus landmark. The east building, being the highest at 15 stories, creates a gateway to the campus, giving the project a distinctive presence on the emerging Mission Bay skyline of San Francisco and acting as a beacon for the east campus entry. Light rail and bus stops are located at this entry.

The south side of the project fronts a large, sun-filled plaza, energized by retail spaces lining the base of the south building. The plaza visually connects along the main axis of the campus to the academic campus green and nearby student center.

Far Left Looking east
Above Looking north
Below East elevation

As part of the campus network of outdoor rooms, the project's west interior garden courtyard remains in the public realm with a slightly elevated plaza holding a Richard Serra sculpture. The gated eastern interior garden courtyard is a private, tree-lined space for the exclusive use of residents. In both public and private outdoor areas the buildings are scaled down with smaller community pavilions and lower profiles to create a greater residential feel and allow more sunlight into the gardens. Community spaces bordering both the public and private realms provide a variety of places to congregate, study, and interact.

FFA performed complete basic design services, including programming, in collaboration with Skidmore, Owings and Merrill of San Francisco.

Upper Left Aerial
Upper Right View from light rail
Lower Left 1st floor plan
Lower Right Bridge detail
Far Right South elevation

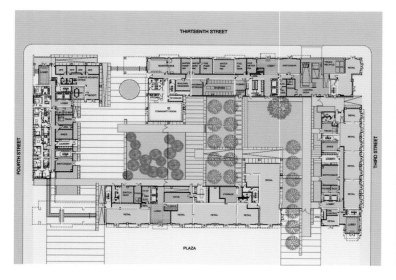

Upper Left Lobby
Upper Right Lobby
Center Left Kitchen
Center Right Living/
dining room
Lower Left
Looking east
Lower Center
Bay windows
Lower Right
Window wall
Far Right
Courtyard entry

Mixed Use

Golden Gateway Commons

San Francisco, California

Golden Gateway Commons is a low-rise, mixed use project located adjacent to the Embarcadero Center at Jackson and Davis Streets in the historic area that was once San Francisco's famous produce district. The project was conceived as an urban, yet private, place to live in the city. A total of 155 condominium residences are dispersed atop two-level commercial office parking podium buildings, resulting in three city blocks of combined openness and landscaping and providing the convenience of in-town living. The residences range in size from 900 to 2,300 square feet; the commercial-office space below totals about 250,000 square feet. Parking is provided for 540 automobiles.

Far Left Aerial waterfront view
Above Plaza level
Below View from park

There are numerous advantages to this "think small" approach, reflected in the highly favorable reaction from various neighborhood environmental groups. The proposal allows that the park and landscaped area are not shadowed by tall buildings; there is no high-rise encroachment on the San Francisco skyline; views of Telegraph Hill residents are not blocked; wind generally generated by tall buildings is avoided; the scale and materials selected are sympathetic to the adjacent older brick buildings of the old market area as well as to historic Jackson Square. Street life is reinforced by the provision of commercial and retail space at street level. Low-rise dwellings have what Jane Jacobs and Oscar Newman call "eyes on the street", tending to prevent vandalism and other street crime.

One of the most significant aspects of this project is that the interests of the developers and environmentalists coincided. Economic and environmental studies all pointed in the same direction, presenting San Franciscans with the uncommon sight of the two groups working together to solve a critical situation successfully.

Far Left Raised plaza
Upper Left and Right Stairs at park
Lower Left Upper level
Lower right South elevation

Wingfield Towers

Reno, Nevada

The Wingfield Towers project is a residential development for the emerging Reno, Nevada market. The highly desirable location is in the heart of Reno, accessible to key transportation corridors, adjacent to the Riverwalk Community and overlooking the Truckee River. An appealing mix of retail at the ground floors of each building will service residents and the community, enhancing the living environment of this destination building. An exceptional amenity package for the residential towers will be offered. The podium plaza will be integrated into the existing Riverwalk and used as a venue for local community festivals and art exhibits.

The development is comprised of 499 high-rise for-sale units and 600 parking spaces. The East Tower has 40 stories and the West Tower has 28 stories above five and one-half levels of parking. Three levels of offices above the podium level are included in the West Tower. A Winter Garden with a 25-yard long lap pool is situated on the top floor of the West Tower for use by residents and guests.

The two towers are connected at the plaza level by an open walkway plaza between the office/commercial uses on the lower floors, as well as onto Island Avenue Riverwalk via a landscaped water feature stairway and elevators. The towers are connected at the pool level by a sky bridge. The subterranean parking structure will have access via Court Street.

Overall, this development makes for a remarkable community asset, particularly for Reno, providing a more upscale and varied mixed use component complementing the already adaptive reuse of several existing buildings into residential developments.

Left Looking west
Below Looking east

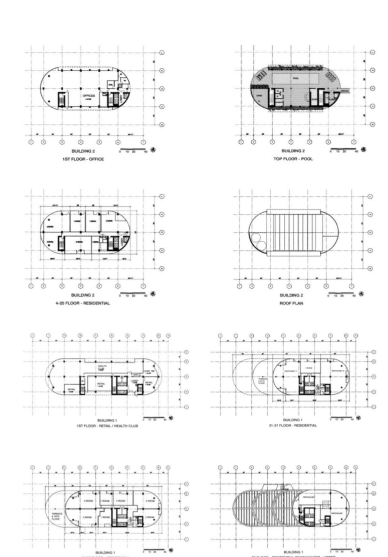

BUILDING 2
1ST FLOOR - OFFICE

BUILDING 2
TOP FLOOR - POOL

BUILDING 2
4-20 FLOOR - RESIDENTIAL

BUILDING 2
ROOF PLAN

BUILDING 1
1ST FLOOR - RETAIL / HEALTH CLUB

BUILDING 1
31-37 FLOOR - RESIDENTIAL

BUILDING 1
18-30 FLOOR - RESIDENTIAL

BUILDING 1
39 FLOOR - RESIDENTIAL TOWNHOUSES - UPPER

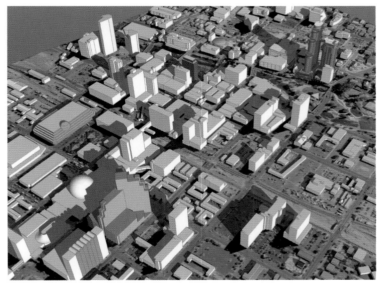

Far Left Looking south
Upper Right Looking north
Center right Aerial View

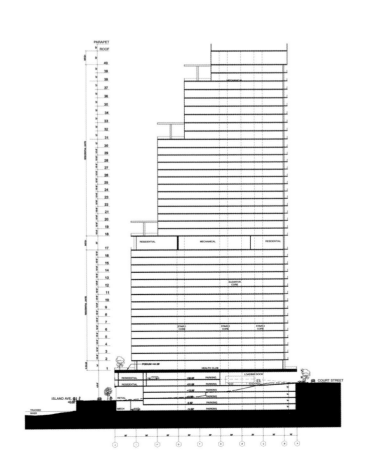

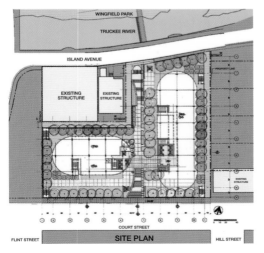

SITE PLAN

Adaptive Re-Use

Oriental Warehouse Lofts

San Francisco, California

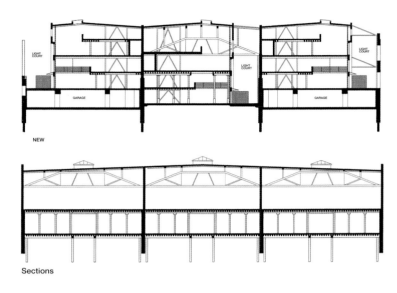

NEW

Sections

Left Looking east from plaza
Below South elevation

Under the San Francisco South Beach Redevelopment Plan of 1981, the Oriental Warehouse was designated an historic landmark due to its historical value as the early arrival point of Oriental immigrants. The brick warehouse, originally built in 1868, with a total area of 88,000 square feet on two floors had for many years been used as a warehouse and storage space.

After nearly a decade of negotiations between historic preservationists and various owners of the building, FFA secured the necessary approvals from the Landmarks Preservation Board and the San Francisco Planning Commission to convert the warehouse into 66 spacious live/work lofts.

The 125-year old brick structure required substantial seismic upgrades and the addition of windows to provide the natural light necessary for residential units. In addition, on the aggregated plan, the adjacent L-shaped property supports an additional 38 unit, five-story structure as well as two 18-story buildings with recreational facilities and some retail space.

Construction of the lofts, which began in late 1995, was completed and all 60 units sold immediately.

Far Left Living room
Upper Left Entry
Upper Right Stairs at entry
Lower Right Kitchen

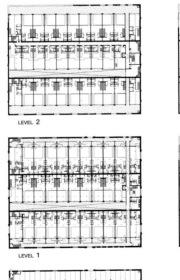

LEVEL 2

LEVEL 4

LEVEL 1

LEVEL 3

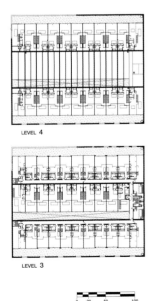

GARAGE

0 20 50 100

High-Rise Apartments

Park Bellevue Tower

Oakland, California

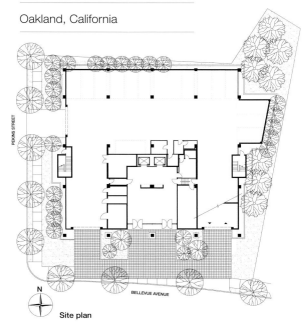

PEKINS STREET

BELLEVUE AVENUE

N

Site plan

Park Bellevue is a 26-story apartment tower built on a one-third acre site on the shore of Lake Merritt in Oakland. Designed in 1964, it was one of the first buildings to employ a computer analyzed steel frame. Sand blasted precast concrete panels cover the columns and beams. The use of this technique enabled the building's structural frame to be dramatically reduced in weight and made the building economically feasible.

Park Bellevue is situated above an underground river that diagonally cuts across the site approximately four and one-half feet below the surface, requiring all parking to be above grade. At first this was thought to be a real detriment to the project; however, the architects were able to turn this requirement into an asset by capitalizing on the view potential of each of the residential units of the tower. Atop the split-level garage is a complete recreational facility with a swimming pool, saunas and game rooms.

Left West elevation
Below 6th floor pool

Above and Far Right Looking east

The tower has 19 residential floors above the recreational level. All balconies on the tower were omitted after a wind analysis demonstrated they would be of only marginal use. Instead of balconies, all residences were correspondingly increased in size. The eyebrows on the building are not, as might be thought, sunshades – they were designed to mitigate the possibly undesirable and uncomfortable physical effects of standing close to very large windows at the edge of the tower. The improved parallax was successful in putting the residents at ease. The building was financed using the FHA's 207 program and was rented at full capacity after completion of construction. In 1985 the building was converted to senior housing. In 1996 it was converted to condominiums.

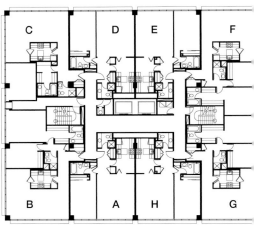

Typical floor plan

South Beach Marina Apartments

San Francisco, California

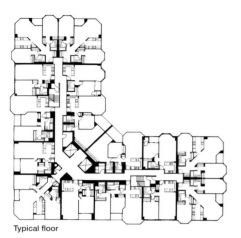

Typical floor

South Beach Marina Apartments is a mixed-use development on a 3.4-acre portion of the block located at the foot of Delancey Street, fronting on the Embarcadero and across from the City's 500 boat marina. The project consists of 414 apartments in four mid-rise buildings. A fifth building was designed as a parking structure for 390 cars with tennis courts located on the roof. The overall project includes a clubhouse and recreation area with swimming pool and spa. At street level, behind the arcade element of the lower buildings, there is 7,900 square feet of commercial space for restaurants and retail establishments to serve residents and the neighborhood.

The structures are reinforced concrete sheer wall building with dryvit clad exteriors. Large bay windows capture the vistas towards the waterfront and Bay Bridge. The apartments are contained in four buildings, two of which are four stories; the third is a thirteen-story tower with a nine-story element; the fourth building is fourteen stories with a nine-story element. The residential units range from 519 square feet one-bedroom units to 1,022 square feet double master bedroom units.

Far Left East tower
Below Looking west

Upper Left Aerial
Upper Right View from entry lobby
Lower Left View from harbor
Lower Right Bay windows
Far Right View from yacht basin

The Avalon at Mission Bay

San Francisco, California

This residential community of 250 housing units is a component of a larger project deemed one of the most significant planning projects in the history of San Francisco. Overall, the project will provide homes for families with low to middle incomes and permanent jobs for over 20,000 people. The existing 313 acres of barren roads and abandoned warehouses are being transformed into a lively new city neighborhood of homes, parks, offices and transit ways, as well as a major UCSF research campus.

A 15-story tower set atop a two-story podium contains 149 dwellings which are typically arranged in a series of 10 apartments per floor; six one-bedroom and four two-bedroom units. The architectural design of the tower emphasizes its verticality, as do the balconies on the southern side overlooking the quiet interior courtyards which capture the afternoon sun. The remaining 91 dwellings are stacked wood-frame flats in a series of three-story structures positioned above a two-story parking garage.

Far left View from light rail
Above Detail
Below Aerial looking west

The flats contain a mixture of studios and one, two and three-bedroom units. The interior parking structure under the flats provides space for 209 cars, two loading spaces and 100 bicycles. The low-rise configuration of the flats offers a pedestrian-friendly entry as well as creating an identity independent of the tower. An interior courtyard of 18,000 square feet of open space allows for pleasant outdoor space for relaxation and interaction amongst the residents.

Wrapping the base of the main structure is 7,800 square feet of retail space, along with resident amenities such as the fitness center and leasing office, and ten loft-style apartments with individual or paired entries. This plan creates an active and attractive neighborhood. FFA was the design architect for this project.

Upper Left Meeting room
Lower Left Fitness center
Far Right View from plaza

Resorts

The Vintage Club

Indian Wells, California

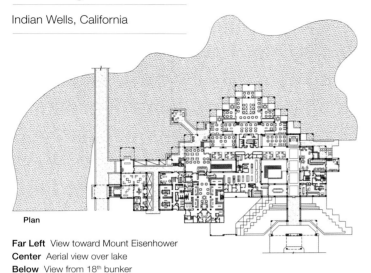

Plan

Far Left View toward Mount Eisenhower
Center Aerial view over lake
Below View from 18th bunker

Following pages View from lake

The clubhouse at Indian Wells occupies a 20-acre site in the exclusive Vintage Club near Palm Springs. Designed to provide members with an elegant, water-oriented facility responsive to the desert environment, the 96,00 square feet two-story concrete and wood frame building is organized on a 24-foot grid forming the matrix for a series of tile-covered pyramidal roofs. The structural frame is expressed in integrally colored concrete with the infill wall areas made of travertine. The building contains dining and banquet facilities to accommodate 1000 people, lounges, locker rooms, a golf pro shop and administrative offices. While enjoying the elegant surroundings of the dining and lounge area, members have an expansive view across a man-made lake to the 18-hole golf course and the mountain range beyond. Members are provided with attendant parking for 363 cars and additional covered parking for 100 golf carts.

The Vintage Swim and Tennis Club, located adjacent to the clubhouse, continues the design theme based on a series of pavilions and pyramid roof forms. Variations on the theme and the use of trellises give the Swim and Tennis Club a separate identity. Terraces and pavilions interwoven among the eleven tennis courts and swimming pool casually integrate indoor and outdoor space. The spatial flow is enhanced by lush landscaping which evokes a feeling of oasis in contrast to the surrounding desert. The café, with extensive outdoor seating, overlooks the sunken championship tennis court and its terraced lawn seating areas.

The Vintage Club was completed in 1981.

Above View from desert
Below Entry

Far Right
Upper Left Tennis pro shop
Center Left Sunken tennis court
Lower Left Swim tennis and fitness center
Upper Right Aerial views
Lower Right Golf pro shop
Bottom Right Sunken tennis courts

Following pages
Clubhouse from golf course

Office/Administration

Dutton Hall

University of California Davis

Davis, California

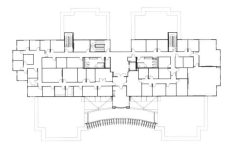

Third floor

Second floor

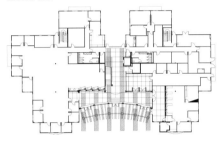

First floor

Dutton Hall is a three-story student administration building. It provides a one-stop center for the growing needs of the numerous offices of the Student Affairs Department, Financial Aid, Student Aid, Accounting, Campus Cashier's office, Learning Skills Center, Student Employment Center, Outreach Services, and Student Judicial Affairs.

The "Hall" represents a significant new structure on campus in that it aesthetically complements the historic central quad. The Hall's design is traditional with a historic feel at the site of the first structures on campus. The Hall has a dramatic, two-story entry lobby and faces a new plaza, a kind of student-oriented "quad" to the west. This outdoor "room" contains ornamental trees, seating and a fountain, creating a pleasant outdoor space accommodating overflow queuing during peak periods of registration as well as informal gatherings.

Cedar shingles are used on the building exterior to complement the two adjacent historic shingle-style buildings constructed in the latter part of the 19th century. The building provides approximately 60,000 square feet of efficient and flexible office space with natural daylight in all permanent work areas.

Left Entry
Below Courtyard elevation

Following pages
Left Entry lobby
Right Collonade and trellis

Civic Executive Center

Walnut Creek, California

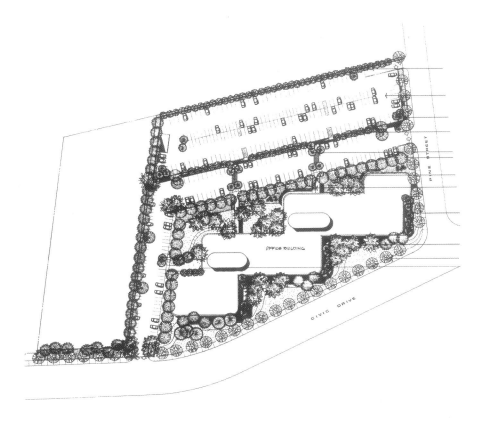

The Civic Executive Center is a three-story, 168,000 square-feet speculative office building with a 400-car parking garage located directly north of Walnut Creek's central business district and within walking distance of BART. To blend in with the neighborhood of small businesses and low-rise housing, a stepped plan was developed to provide large planting pockets along Civic Drive. These setbacks, in combination with third floor terraces, help to achieve a scale suitable for the neighborhood.

While the street side landscape, with its bermed entrance plaza, is treated as a formal setting for the building, the west side has an informal exterior patio and garden for office workers. The west side is also the primary entrance to the building. Two bridges link the lobbies directly to the parking structure and give access to the middle level of the three-story building. An open stair in the lobby connects the first two floors and provides visual interest. The serpentine building's exterior is clear anodized aluminum and gray-tinted reflective glass. Windows are full height on the north elevation, and two-thirds height on the balance of the building to minimize heating and cooling loads while providing spectacular views of Mount Diablo and the surrounding hills. The radiused corners provide the building with a pleasing aspect to the passing motorist while reducing the apparent bulk.

Left View toward bridge
Below Stair to bus stop

Left Lobby and stair
Above Curved exterior

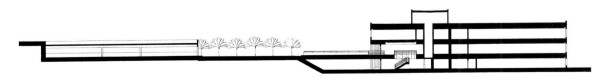

TRANSVERSE SECTION AT CORE NO. 1

Emeryville City Hall

Emeryville, California

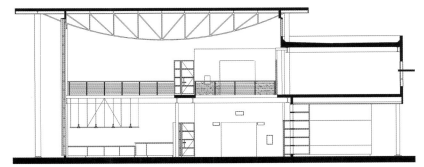

Section

The City of Emeryville commissioned FFA to produce a Civic Center Master Plan for interim and future build-out of an entire city block bounded by Park Avenue, Hollis, Haven and 40th Streets.

The plan involved rehabilitating the historic 7,500-square foot old town hall built in 1903 and designing a new 20,000-square foot building for administrative offices and multi-purpose areas. Site planning, internal and external circulation and the creation of a strong civic presence were all important issues.

Final build-out included the construction of additional structure (i.e. new Council Chambers, office space expansion, a community theater and facilities, structured parking and air rights developments) and open spaces identified as part of the public master planning process.

The planning and design process included a series of workshops and meetings with the Project Committee, neighborhood and citizen groups, as well as consultants and staff. The overall framework for public participation and decision-making was an integral part of the master planning and City Hall design process. Consensus-building streamlined the overall design process and proved more efficient project scheduling and budgeting.

Left Entry
Below North elevation

Following pages
Left South entry
Right View from courtyard

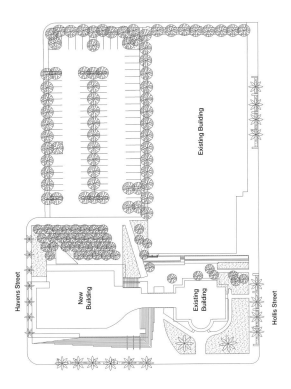

Site plan

Far Left Above East elevation
Far Left Below South elevation
Upper Right Council chamber
Center Right Main stairs at lobby

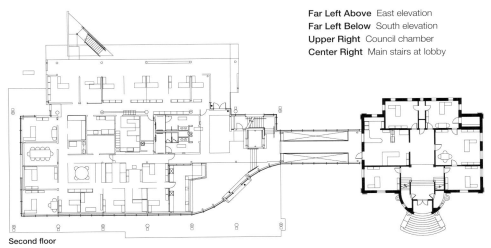

Second floor

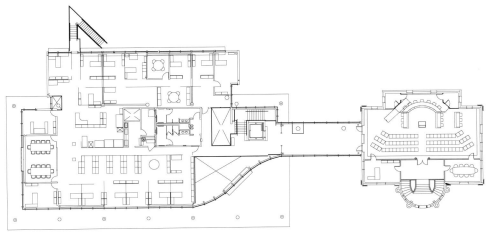

First floor

Institutional

Chabot Observatory and Science Center

Oakland, California

The Chabot Observatory and Science Center is a replacement for the historic observatory built in the twenties. The new site is 13.5 acres located on a ridge at 1,540 feet above sea level. The new facility is about 81,000 square feet.

FFA was selected as the design architect. Design drawings were completed in the fall of 1996, whereupon the office of Gerson/Overstreet continued with construction documents.

The sponsors of this project adopted the concept of providing an observatory in the widest sense – from microscopic to cosmic. There are facilities for presenting and observing nature at all scales. A new 240-seat planetarium and a new domed projection IMAX theater are of key interest. Ample space for exhibits is provided. The historical late 19th century 20-inch and 8-inch refractor telescopes have been relocated here. There is a complement of new telescopes and equipment.

The purpose of the facility, in addition to providing celestial observing capabilities for amateur and professional astronomers and college students, is to provide teacher training in the sciences, educational facilities for primary and secondary students, and educational facilities for the general public.

Included are the following: a Physics and Chemistry Lab; a student Bio-Lab; a Discovery Lab; an Environ Lab; and a Computer Lab. Education resources include a multimedia studio to produce and send videos to Oakland schools.

The Chabot Observatory and Science Center opened to the public in August of 2000.

Far Left Aerial looking northeast
Upper Left Planetarium
Below Exterior detail

Next Page
Left Telescope domes
Right Courtyard elevation

Following Page Left
Upper Left Curtain wall at stairs
Upper Right Observation point at bridge
Lower Left View of the stairs looking down
Lower Right View of the stairs looking up

Following Page Right Exterior platform at IMAX theatre

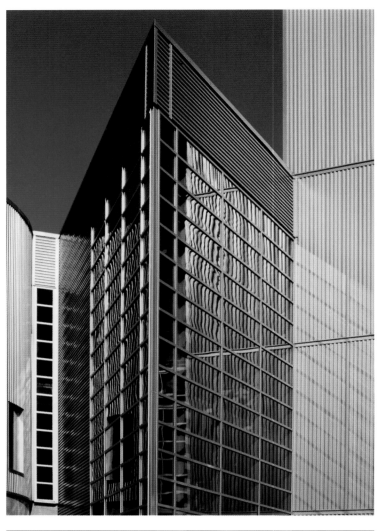

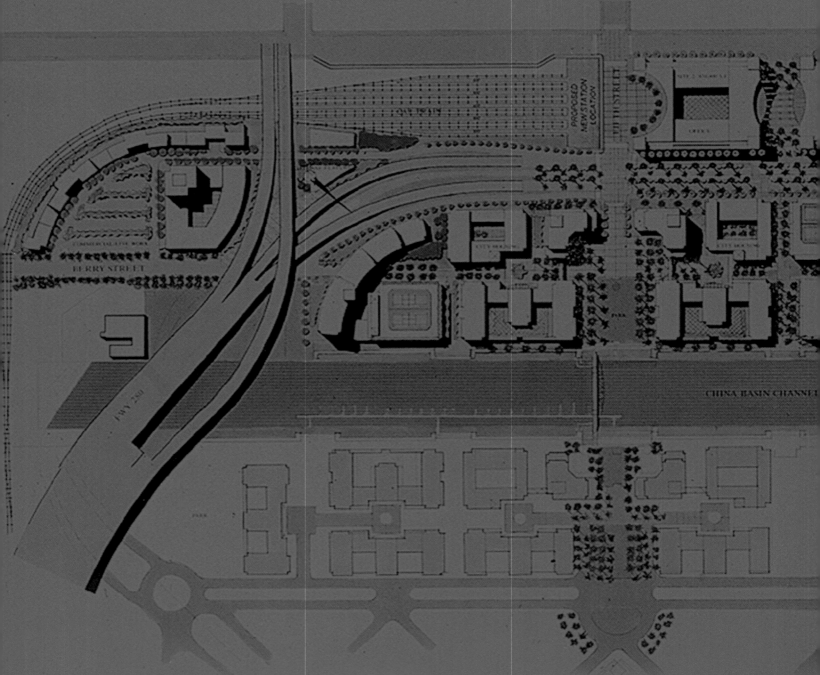

Masterplanning

Imperial Bay Master Plan

Weehawken and

West New York, New Jersey

This 265-acre waterfront project is located along the New Jersey shore of the Hudson River at the base of the palisades opposite Manhattan and in both the towns of Weehawken and West New York. The Lincoln Tunnel passes under the southerly end of the project and the northern end is opposite 75th Street in Manhattan. The project is to be developed incrementally over 30 years: starting with the Town Center and Harbor, then extending north and south along an axial waterfront boulevard. At ultimate build-out there will be approximately 12,000 housing units, 12,000,000 square feet of office space, 600,000 square feet of retail and a 420-room hotel.

The development plan arranges circulation and building massing to take advantage of the two primary attributes of the site – views to the Manhattan skyline and the strong marine orientation. The plan was developed in collaboration with Cesar Pelli & Associates and Jonathan Barnett. Two parallel landscaped boulevards traverse the plan north and south, crossed by secondary streets at regular city block intervals in alignment with the existing streets above the Palisades. This pattern creates view corridors for the existing towns and replicates the towns' scale. One diagonal boulevard interrupts the grid leading from the Palisades and terminates at the river edge and the southern portion of the Town Center. The Town Center, the heart of the development, is located at the widest point of the site and includes a major public open space and a ferry terminal and harbor on the Hudson River.

The transportation plan includes a light-rail system in addition to the vehicular and pedestrian systems and the ferry to Manhattan at 38th Street. The light rail system runs north-south the length of the project, with an interchange to the proposed east-west shuttle train connecting the Town Center, through the old Conrail tunnel, to the regional systems west of the project.

Far Left Residential piers over Hudson River
Above Ferry Landing
Below Model of master plan

BC Place

Vancouver, British Columbia

The site for this 224-acre development encompasses the entire southern waterfront of downtown Vancouver, facing the False Creek inlet. This site possesses a number of positive attributes, including two miles of waterfront oriented to the south, views of False Creek and English Bay, distant views to the mountains, a direct connection to downtown and access to waterfront pedestrian walks.

Project planning was executed in collaboration with Arthur Erickson Architects of Vancouver and with the extensive involvement of Vancouver City staff and personnel from the Provincial Government of British Columbia.

At ultimate build-out in the year 2010 the development contains approximately 10,000 dwelling units, 3.5 million square feet of offices, 3.5 million square feet of mixed-use commercial and retail space, 900,000 square feet of hotel space, 49 acres of park land, a 70,000 seat domed stadium, a provincial park with museums and amphitheater, six marinas (1,100 berths) and marine support facilities, community facilities and schools. The careful clustering of the building masses in the form of peaks and valleys assures views of the city, water, and the mountains beyond.

Left Model photo
Below Stadium

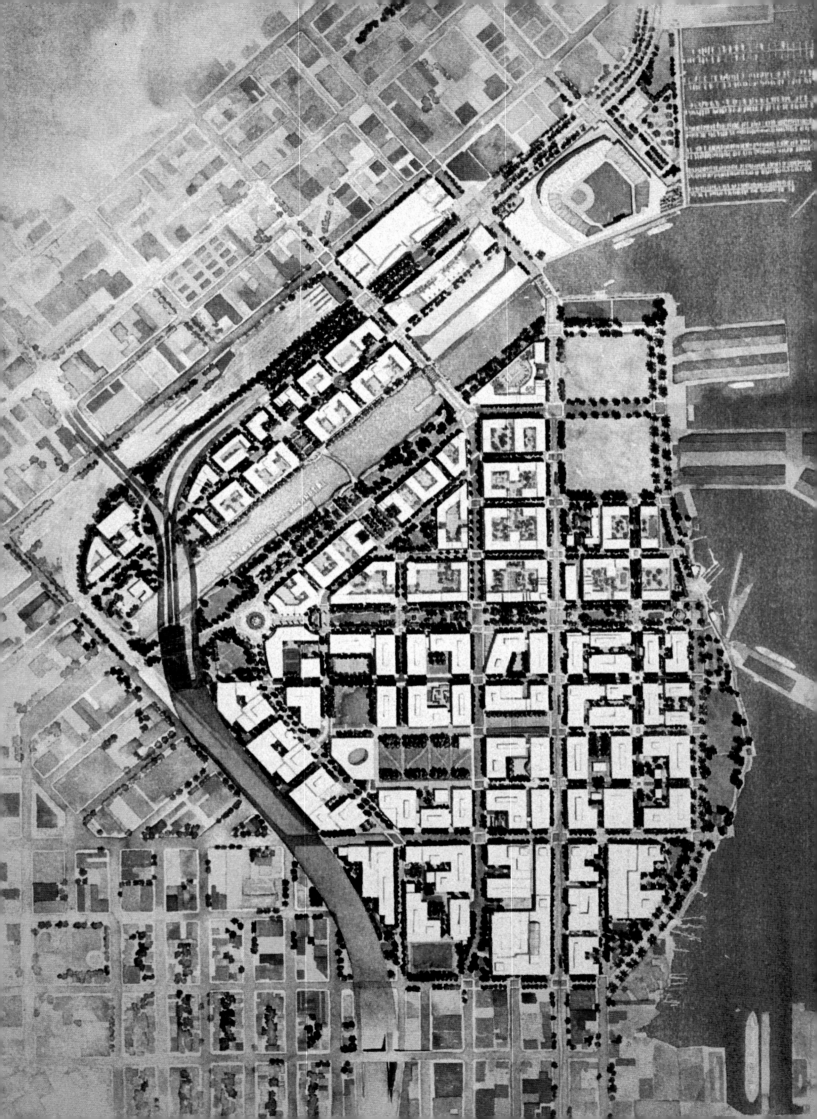

Mission Bay Master Plan

San Francisco, California

Mission Bay encompasses 313 acres and is under the jurisdiction of the City and County of San Francisco with participation from Catellus Development as the project sponsor. The Mission Bay plan area is about one mile south of San Francisco's Financial District, on both north and south sides of the China Basin Channel. It is bordered by the South of Market, Showplace Square, North Potrero, Potrero Hill, the Central Bayfront and San Francisco Bay. The boundaries are Townsend Street on the north, Seventh Street and Interstate 80 on the west, Mariposa Street on the south and China Basin and Third Streets on the east.

After decades of an interactive planning process, public dialogue, meetings, information exchange, newsletters, forums, issue-oriented small group meetings, open design studio hours, citizen review of preliminary draft reports, and environmental impact report scoping, the plan has matured into a vibrant neighborhood community for the city of San Francisco. The result is a plan that incorporates many of the values and needs articulated by the public process.

Mission Bay represents an unprecedented opportunity to develop state-of-the-art facilities within what will become the preeminent biomedical research center in the country. As home to UCSF's new 43-acre, 2.65 million-square foot research and teaching campus, Mission Bay offers a science-driven environment encouraging public-private alliances.

Mission Bay is currently in different construction and planning phases for the new Life Sciences Campus, UCSF's Research Campus and the Corporate, Science and Technology Development Campus. Also planned is a 500 room hotel, 850,000 square feet of retail space, 6,000 residential units and 49 acres of parks and open space.

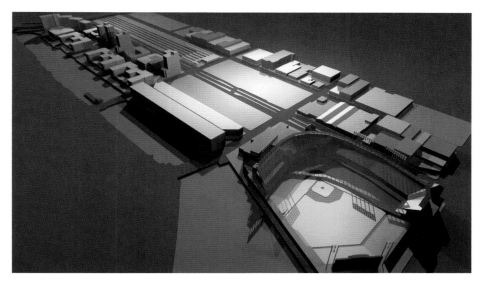

Far left Mission Bay Master Plan
Above North Channel
Below North Channel plan

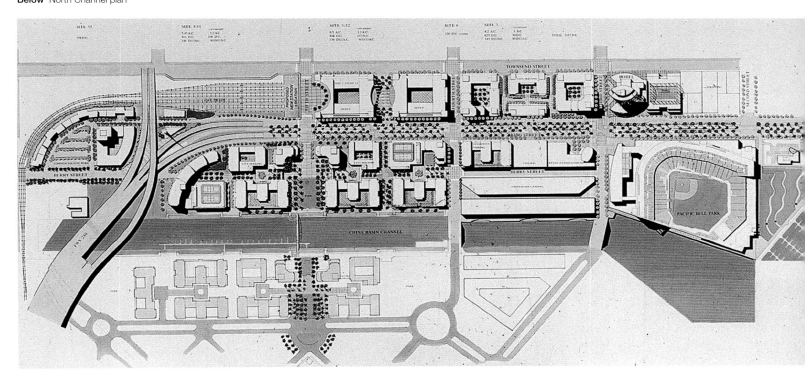

San Ramon City Center Master Plan

San Ramon, California

FFA, as executive and design architects, with the office of Ellerbe Becket as consultant architects, was commissioned to master plan the 290,000-square foot San Ramon City Center. The program includes offices and council chambers, a library, a center for the arts, theater, children's museum, retail development, gallery and meeting rooms, a pedestrian bridge and a parking structure. Pending approval, the program may also include an Olympic aquatic center.

FFA jumpstarted the project by coordinating key "brainstorming" sessions with city council members, translating the program into building footprints and conducting numerous workshops to gather public opinion in an effort to transform the desires and ideas of the community into the "San Ramon City Center Vision".

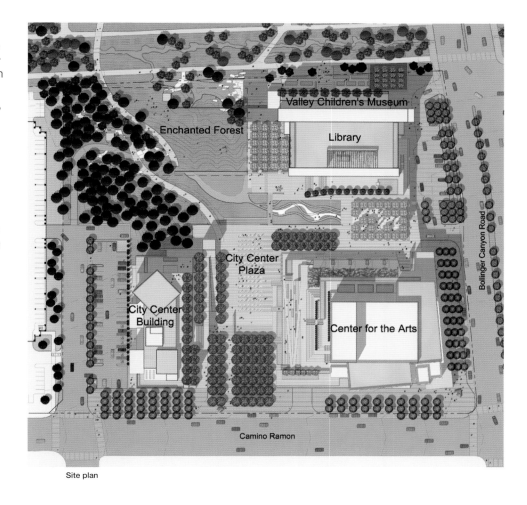

Site plan

Left San Ramon City Center
Above Right Site plan
Below View from park

Piedmont Civic Center Master Plan

Piedmont, California

The city of Piedmont selected FFA as the visionary design and planning consultant to integrate the community's needs for recreational, cultural and social amenities with existing municipal and educational facilities. The Civic Center Master Plan encompasses both facilities design and development of circulation solutions within the four square block civic center footprint. The initial public process identified a desire for offices, meeting spaces, classrooms, a performing arts venue, swimming pools, a recreation center, parking and other potential facilities.

FFA conducted scoping meetings, community workshops, vision sessions and City Council updates in preparation of the Civic Center Master Plan final document. This plan improves the unique and mixed-use area which is a community asset, reflects the high density concerns of the community, establishes consistent design principles throughout the Civic Center, provides public recreational space, emphasizes safety and access, addresses parking needs and is consistent with the General Plan.

Left Above Plaza
Left Below City center plan
Above Right Swim and fitness center
Below Master plan

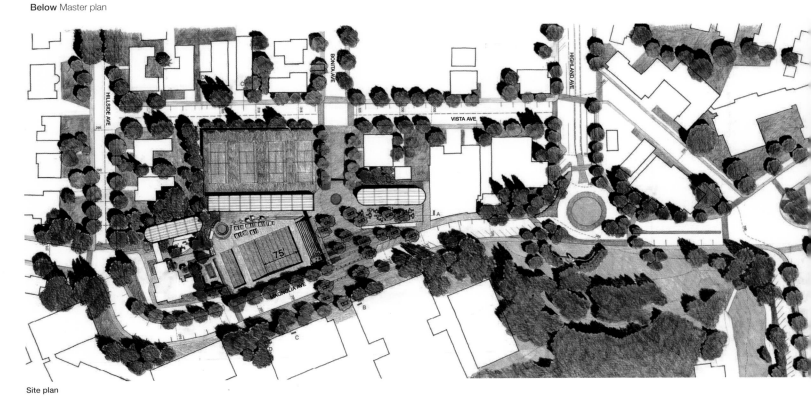

Site plan

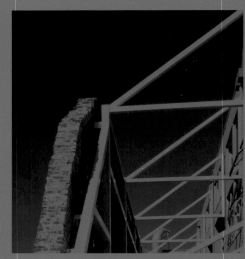

ORO *editions*

Publishers of Architecture, Art, Design and Photography

Gordon Goff - Publisher

USA: PO Box 998, Pt Reyes Station, CA 94956

Asia: Block 8, Lorong Bakar Batu #02-04, Singapore 348743

www.oroeditions.com
info@oroeditions.com

Copyright © 2010 by ORO *editions*

ISBN: 978-0-9820607-0-4

Graphic Design

Andrés Rodríguez Ruiz, Sally Roydhouse

Production

Joanne Tan, Davina Tjandra, Andrés Rodríguez Ruiz

Color Separation and Printing

ORO *editions*, Singapore

Model Making

Rami Geller

Photographs

Joe Aker, Morley Baer, Richard Barnes, Charles Callister, A Robert Fisher, Joshua Friewald,
Rodney Friedman, Nobu Kaji, Carlo Macaione, Russell McMasters, Glen Mitchell, J D Peterson,
Photo Stephenson, Steve Proehl (Aerials), Eric Sahlin, Mark Steppan, Matthew Steppan, Strode Eckert,
Steve Whittaker

Renderings and Sketches

John Francis Marsh, SWA, Michael Schaefer

We have made every effort to minimize the carbon footprint of this project. In pursuit of this goal, ORO *editions*, in
association with Global ReLeaf, has arranged to plant two trees for each and every tree used in the manufacturing
of the FSC paper produced for this book. Global ReLeaf is an international campaign run by American Forests, the
nation's oldest nonprofit conservation organization. Global ReLeaf is American Forests' education and action program
that helps individuals, organizations, agencies, and corporations improve the local and global environment by planting
and caring for trees.

Printed in China

North American and International Distribution:

Publishers Group West
1700 Fourth Street
Berkeley, CA 94710
USA

www.pgw.com